D0330842

A Gift For:

Rylie Morgan

From:

Grandma & Papaw
2021

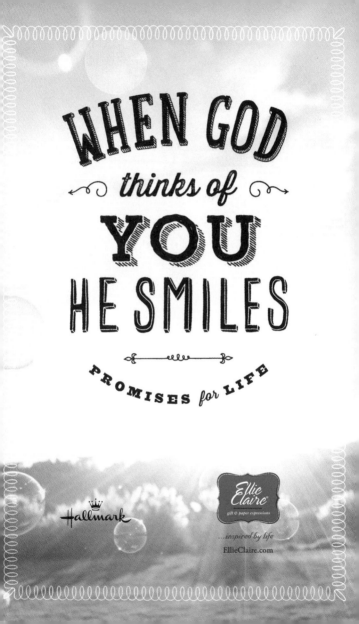

WHEN GOD

thinks of

YOU

HE SMILES

PROMISES *for* LIFE

Hallmark

Ellie Claire
gift & paper expressions

...inspired by life
EllieClaire.com

This edition published in 2018 by Hallmark Gift Books, a division of Hallmark Cards, Inc., Kansas City, MO 64141 under license from Ellie Claire, an imprint of Worthy Media, Inc.

Visit us on the Web at Hallmark.com.

Scripture quotations are taken from the following sources: The Holy Bible, King James Version (KJV). The Holy Bible, New International Version®, NIV® Copyright © 1973, 1978, 1984, 2011 by Biblica, Inc.® All rights reserved worldwide. The Holy Bible, New King James Version® (NKJV). Copyright © 1982 by Thomas Nelson, Inc. The Holy Bible, English Standard Version® (ESV®), copyright © 2001 by Crossway Bibles, a publishing ministry of Good News Publishers. The New American Standard Bible® (NASB), Copyright © 1960, 1962, 1963, 1968, 1971, 1972, 1973, 1975, 1977, 1995 by The Lockman Foundation. The Holy Bible, New Living Translation (NLT) copyright © 1996, 2004, 2007 by Tyndale House Foundation. Used by permission of Tyndale House Publishers Inc., Carol Stream, Illinois 60188. *The Message* (MSG). Copyright © 1993, 1994, 1995, 1996, 2000, 2001, 2002. Used by permission of NavPress Publishing Group. *The Living Bible* (TLB) copyright © 1971 by Tyndale House Foundation. Used by permission of Tyndale House Publishers Inc., Carol Stream, Illinois 60188. Used by permission. All rights reserved.

Written by Jennifer Geralds.
Edited by Jill Jones.
Cover and interior photos from stocksy.com.
Cover and interior design by Gearbox | StudioGearbox.com.
Typesetting by Jeff Jansen | AestheticSoup.net

ISBN: 978-1-63059-736-8
1BOK1420

Made in China.
0920

MAY THE Lord

bless you and protect you.

May the Lord smile on you

and be gracious to you.

NUMBERS 6:24-25 NLT

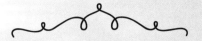

It can happen in the smallest of moments: When your child reaches up to hold your hand. When a shooting star flashes across the night sky. When you wake up and realize you have several more hours you can sleep. These little everyday events light up your heart and your face and another miracle happens: you smile!

But did you know that all of these precious life moments hidden neatly throughout your day are not mere accidents or even coincidences? You, dear child of God, have a heavenly Father who has giftwrapped each of these treasures for you to discover. Why? Because your delight makes God smile.

In fact, *you* make God smile! On your up days and your down. On good hair days and bad. When you're serving and singing and blessing others, and when you feel like hiding from the rest of humanity. God's answer to you is always yes! So no matter what today holds, remember your Father is holding you in His everlasting arms, and smile!

Because God already is.

ALL THAT
WE HAVE AND ARE

is one of the unique and
never-to-be-repeated ways God
has chosen to express Himself
in space and time.

EACH OF US,

made in His image and likeness,
is yet another promise
He has made to the universe
that He will continue to love
it and care for it.

BRENNAN MANNING

BLOOMING BLESSINGS

❦ ⎯⎯ ⁓⁓⁓ ⎯⎯ ❧

I am a rose of Sharon, a lily of the valleys.

SONG OF SOLOMON 2:1 NIV

You have waited for months since you first tilled the soil. Patiently, you praised the tender green shoot as it straightened itself from the ground beneath. With bated breath, you watched for the great unfolding, that wonderful moment when its delicate petals broke from the bud to color your world with fragrance and beauty. All because you know—from the lowly dandelion and the wild wisteria to the awesome orchid—that every bloom is a blessing from God, a small explosion of Creator glory.

But did you know that God sees you like a beautiful flower? He prepared the soil, your life as you've experienced it. He has watered and watched and cared for you as you've grown, waiting with great anticipation for the moment your full beauty would unfurl. You were planned and planted to make the world a more colorful place. To fill it with the fragrance of a master Gardener's love. Your shape, your timing, your palette, your purpose—all are perfect. Celebrate the beautiful person you are, and give glory to the God who made you that way!

The king is lying on his couch, enchanted by the fragrance of my perfume.

SONG OF SOLOMON 1:12 NLT

As we grow in our capacities to see and enjoy the joys that God has placed in our lives, life becomes a glorious experience of discovering His endless wonders.

COFFEE KISS

❧ ⸻ ❦

The LORD gives grace and glory;
no good thing does He withhold from those who walk uprightly.

PSALM 84:11 NASB

There it is. No matter how pleasant the music you select, the dreaded sound from your alarm clock signals the end of sleep and the start of a new day. Lying in bed, you wonder what the day will hold, looking for that extra motivation you need to not hit the snooze button one more time. And then the thought comes. *Coffee*. Yes, now you can smell it even from where you are (and you're so glad you remembered to set that timer!). It's just the jolt of energy you know you need to face whatever comes your way.

So while you enjoy your morning java, thank God for giving you His special gift. God, who planned the coffee plant and all its special aromas. God, who gave some farmer the insight needed to roast and crush and steep those curious beans until the delightful effect of coffee was discovered. All this goodness comes from God, straight to the ones He loves and lives to energize with His very own presence. This morning, your coffee is God's wake-up kiss to greet His world with eyes that see His loving hand in every good thing.

Every good thing given and every perfect gift is from above, coming down from the Father of lights, with whom there is no variation or shifting shadow.

JAMES 1:17 NASB

Dear Lord, grant me the grace of wonder. Surprise me, amaze me, awe me in every crevice of Your universe.... Each day enrapture me with Your marvelous things without number. I do not ask to see the reason for it all; I ask only to share the wonder of it all.

JOSHUA ABRAHAM HESCHEL

EGGSTRA SPECIAL

You will fill me with joy in your presence,
with eternal pleasures at your right hand.

PSALM 16:11 NIV

You can fry it. Scramble it. Or put it in a cake. You can make custards or quiches or even soufflés if you're skilled enough. In fact, eggs are one of the most versatile, useful, and plentiful protein sources on our planet. Who would have ever thought that something so gooey-slimy and strange could be such a lifesaver?

God, that's who. God, the One who conceived the idea, giddy with all the Easter-dyeing, dessert-making, life-changing potential He had hidden in its perfectly crafted casing. He couldn't wait for us to discover all its uses. Maybe there's more yet to come!

But God has hidden something else inside that shell. It's the story of life. Your life. Every oval orb is a reminder of God's magnificent plan all packed into your fragile-yet-firm frame. He has filled you with all kinds of potential, and He is eager to see all the ways He can use you to make life sweeter and better—for you and others. Don't worry if your life looks a little messy (like the inside of that egg). It's the stuff God uses to make the most spectacular delights.

Is this not laid up in store with Me, sealed up among My treasures?

DEUTERONOMY 32:34 NKJV

Cry out for insight, and ask for understanding. Search for them as you would for silver; seek them like hidden treasures.

PROVERBS 2:3–4 NLT

God has a wonderful plan for each person He has chosen. He knew even before He created this world what beauty He would bring forth from our lives.

LOUISE B. WYLY

MOONLIGHT GLADNESS

❦ ⸺ ⚬⚬⚬ ⸺ ❧

You are the light of the world.

MATTHEW 5:14 NKJV

Have you ever wondered what the world would be like without the moon's soft glow? No gilded leaves to light your evening walk. No romantic gleam on late-night conversations. No sparkle on the dark ocean's tide. It's as if God just knew: we need different kinds of light for life. The brilliant blaze of the sun is perfect for day, but sometimes our souls need something softer.

You too glow with a radiance that comes from your Creator. At times, you are bold and bright, shining light into the darkened places. You feel on fire, powerful, poised to change the world. But evenings do come. And like embers after the fire, your warmth burns deeper, glows softer, filling the night with a more peaceful perspective. You become an open invitation to all those around you to warm themselves and rest.

Thank God for shades of light! Whether you feel fully stoked right now or just slowly simmering after all the activity, rejoice in the God who literally gave you the moon…and with it, the power to glow with His glory day and night.

Praise Him, sun and moon; praise Him, all you stars of light!

PSALM 148:3 NKJV

Hope, like the gleaming taper's light,
Adorns and cheers our way;
And still, as darker grows the night,
Emits a brighter ray.

OLIVER GOLDSMITH

SUN-KISSED STROLL

Before the mountains were brought forth, or ever You had formed the earth and the world, even from everlasting to everlasting, you are God.

PSALM 90:2 NKJV

Coarse sand rubs bare feet as the cool, soothing wash of morning's tide tickles and refreshes every step. The sound of playful sea gulls, diving, soaring, calling out into the warm breeze, calms your soul, even as your heart races with your pace. Breathing in the fresh, salty air, you realize, at least for a moment, that life is good. God is good. His embrace feels as warm as the sun on your skin.

Can you see the horizon? That long line in the distance where blue sky kisses the sea and land? It circles around you, giving you a glimpse of the endless nature of God's love and glory. He made this day. This sand beneath your feet. The sea and all its infinite creatures. The salt and the sun. And He made it for you—even for this very moment. He wants you to see with your eyes, hear with your ears, taste with your tongue, and feel with your skin the incredible depth of His delight in you.

It *is* all good! So soak it all in and smile, because you are loved.

How precious also are Your thoughts to me, O God! How great is the sum of them! If I should count them, they would be more in number than the sand.

PSALM 139:17–18 NKJV

You alone are the LORD; You have made heaven…the earth and everything on it, the seas and all that is in them, and You preserve them all.

NEHEMIAH 9:6 NKJV

Hope floods my heart with delight!
Running on air, mad with life, dizzy, reeling.
Upward I mount—faith is sight, life is feeling.
Hope is the day-star of might!

MARGARET WITTER FULLER

HEALING HUGS

—— • ——

I was thrust into your arms at my birth.
You have been my God from the moment I was born.

PSALM 22:10 NLT

It started when you were a baby, the comfort of bundled blankets wrapped around you for warmth. Instinctively, you sensed your mother's arms, your father's voice, relaxing in the security of their embrace. From then on, every bump and bruise simply felt better if you could just feel that encouraging hug, the closeness of a loved one lending strength into your world.

But how does God hug His kids? If you reach your arms up, you only feel the seemingly empty air. *I wish God could just give me a squeeze,* you think to yourself.

And then you feel it: That sudden, encouraging text from a friend. That kind smile from your spouse. A clasp around your legs by your little one. God's hugs are coming to you from every direction. From the checkbook that miraculously balanced to the neighbor who stopped by to drop off garden vegetables, God has wrapped your life tightly with His love to bundle you close to His heart. Realize His presence all around you, and hug Him right back with a heart full of thanks and hands that reach out to help others feel the warmth of God's hugs, too.

The eternal God is your refuge, and his everlasting arms are under you.

DEUTERONOMY 33:27 NLT

He is everything that is good and comfortable for us.
He is our clothing that for love wraps us, clasps us,
and all surrounds us for tender love.

JULIAN OF NORWICH

RIPPLE EFFECT

It is God who works in you both to will and to do for His good pleasure.

PHILIPPIANS 2:13 NKJV

It doesn't matter how far you throw it. One minute the water is a mirror, still as stone, reflecting white clouds and blue sky, the tall, colorful trees lining the edges. Then enters the rock. A single shot into the center of stillness, and the picture comes to life. Wave after symmetrical wave rolls out from the epicenter of action, pulsing energy that races out in all directions until it spills onto the lake's sandy shore. It's amazing how one pebble can release so much power.

You, at times, may feel like a simple stone, lining the shore of a place much bigger than you. Powerless, perhaps, to make an impact in this sea of billions of people and places.

But remember the ripple effect. When God throws you into the mix He has made, He throws with precision and purpose. You were made for impact. You, bearer of His glory, will give off an energy that only comes from Him. And it will roll out from you, unstoppable as the waves in the sea. The power of God's love in you is destined for effect—even to the ends of the earth. You will change the face of the world!

Like your name, O God, your praise reaches to the ends of the earth.

PSALM 48:10 NIV

Recognizing who we are in Christ and aligning our life
with God's purpose for us gives a sense of destiny....
It gives form and direction to our life.

JEAN FLEMING

GOD'S SUNSHINE

―――⚜―――

For great is your love, reaching to the heavens;
your faithfulness reaches to the skies.

PSALM 57:10 NIV

Walking down the road, you pull your sleeves over your hands, tuck your head down, and wrap your arms around your body, fighting to find some warmth. *I hate the cold*, you think to yourself, as your body sends out another shiver from head to toe. But suddenly, a small miracle breaks through the clouds above. Sun, warm and golden, hiding for what has seemed forever, is suddenly shining. Its rays reach down to your freezing frame and kiss your face with light and welcome warmth. *Ahhhhh, that's much better*, you think to yourself, face now upturned. *If only it will stay!*

As the sun warms your skin, let God's message of love sink deeper into your soul. He knows life gets clouded over with worries and work. He understands how burdens are hard to bear. But He is not gone. Like the sun, He is only hidden, waiting for His perfect moment to break through the gloom with His mercy and grace. He beckons us to seek shelter in His great embrace. So turn your face upward and feel the warmth of His heart flood your body from head to toe, and know—His love for you stays forever.

To you who fear My name the Sun of Righteousness shall arise with healing in His wings.

MALACHI 4:2 NKJV

Do not be afraid to enter the cloud that is settling down on your life. God is in it. The other side is radiant with His glory.

L. B. COWMAN

SMILING BACK

May the LORD bless you and protect you.
May the LORD smile on you and be gracious to you.

NUMBERS 6:24 NLT

You're rubbing your hands together, eyes downcast. You're nervous, and you wish you could calm the rising tempest in your chest as you wonder whether or not your invitation will be accepted. But then you look up and see it on her face.

The flicker in the eye. The creases in the cheek. Lips part, teeth shine, and a beautiful smile erupts—the sign that all is well. *It's going to be okay!* You have been accepted. Appreciated. Your risk was met with reward, and you feel the rush of calm that comes with successful connection. You can't help but answer back with a smile of your own.

Have you ever wondered why God gave our faces the

funny ability to smile? No matter what the culture, this simple gesture speaks the same language: You are accepted and valued. You matter and your presence enters joy into the equation.

Even though we can't see God's face on this side of heaven, we see the laugh-lines of His heart lining other people's faces. May every smile you see today remind you to be brave. Look up to your Father and behold His beaming face. You are loved. Accepted. And your heart can't help but smile back.

When I smiled at them, they scarcely believed it;
the light of my face was precious to them.

JOB 29:24 NIV

Love is the response of the heart to the overwhelming goodness of God.... You may be so awestruck and full of love at His presence that words do not come.

RICHARD J. FOSTER

JOYS COME FROM

simple and natural things:

mists over meadows,

sunlight on leaves,

the path of the moon over water.

SIGURD F. OLSON

LIKE A DIAMOND

*There has never been the slightest doubt in my mind that the God
who started this great work in you would keep at it and bring
it to a flourishing finish on the very day Christ Jesus appears.*

PHILIPPIANS 1:6 MSG

Have you ever seen an actual diamond in the rough? Not
the cliché, the real deal—the sight that diamond min-
ers long to see. It looks so amazingly UNspectacular. Un-
impressive. Unattractive. Worthless—*unless* you have been
trained to look for the value hidden deeper inside. The
ignorant only see the ugly, black outside. Professionals
see the potential, the priceless treasure that lies within.

And so, you've probably heard people called diamonds in the rough, meaning that with a little polish,
they might become a little more presentable to the world.
But God wants you to know that He sees something better
than a diamond deep down. He sees all your potential, the

very best you can be. With His help, you can be more sensational than your mind can even conceive. So special, in fact, that His angels wait in eager anticipation to witness your awesomeness unveiled.

So the next time you look in the mirror and find the image lacking, or you start to grow weary with the weight of imperfection, leave it to the Professional to determine your worth. God, who designed you to sparkle with His divine glory, is polishing and perfecting you for the day when your true beauty will be fully revealed to heaven's delight.

Beloved, now we are children of God; and it has not yet been revealed what we shall be, but we know that when He is revealed, we shall be like Him, for we shall see Him as He is.

1 JOHN 3:2 NKJV

May our lives be illumined by the steady radiance renewed daily, of a wonder, the source of which is beyond reason.

DAG HAMMARSKJÖLD

ETERNITY'S DREAMCHILD

I knew you before you were formed within your mother's womb; before you were born I sanctified you and appointed you as my spokesman to the world.

JEREMIAH 1:5 TLB

The world boasts to house over six billion people. Can you imagine trying to keep track of all those faces, those names, those life stories? The magnitude of it all can be overwhelming. Your own significance comes into question. Can a single life, like a drop of water in the ocean, really matter?

God says you are no ordinary raindrop. You are chosen. Planned. Accounted for…from before time even began! You were in God's mind and heart before a single plant graced the face of the earth. Before the sun even rose to shine. Before the first sound of laughter filled the air.

You were God's smile, the pleasure of His creation. He knew it was good. Master storyteller that He is, He waited patiently for the perfect reveal, the moment your special life should be made known to the world.

Can a single life matter? It certainly does when it is crafted and planned by the God of creation. He made you for this very moment, to be a blessing and beacon of hope to light the world around you.

He chose us in him before the creation of the world
to be holy and blameless in his sight.

EPHESIANS 1:4 NIV

God not only knows us, but He values us highly in spite of all He
knows.... You and I are the creatures He prizes above the rest
of His creation. We are made in His image, and He sacrificed
His Son that each one of us might be one with Him.

JOHN FISHER

BOOK ENDS

⚜ ‿‿‿ ⚜

I am God, and there is none like me, declaring the end from the beginning and from ancient times things not yet done, saying, "My counsel shall stand, and I will accomplish all my purpose."

ISAIAH 46:9–10 ESV

You know you have other things to do. You should do. But you just can't do. Not right now, anyway. You've *got* to finish that page. Well, maybe one more chapter. Okay, one more book in that incredibly addictive series. Those characters are like your family! Their world is now yours, and life just won't feel right until you know how it all ends. But when it finally does (as the last page is turned), a strange and sudden sadness taints even the happiest ever after. That world of wonder seems forever lost. It seems we were created to enjoy and experience great stories, just not for forever endings.

Every good book you read hints at the plot God is writing into your very real life. Your birth and life so far was not chapter one. God plotted you in His outline before history ever began. But you have now entered the work, graced with every good feature He wanted to thicken the plot and propel His masterful plan forward. Your life is no accident, but instead, an intricately woven thread in His masterpiece of glory. So read every day with wonder-filled eyes. God's epic love story is beyond sensational. Better still, His *happily-ever-after* has no end.

Like an open book, you watched me grow from conception to birth;
all the stages of my life were spread out before you,
the days of my life all prepared before I'd even lived one day.

PSALM 139:16 MSG

Every person's life is a fairy tale written by God's fingers.

HANS CHRISTIAN ANDERSEN

IMAGE THAT

—⚜—

*Now to him who is able to do immeasurably more than
all we ask or imagine...to him be glory!*

EPHESIANS 3:20–21 NIV

Y ou don't mean to do it. You think you're focused on
the task at hand. But before you know it, your thoughts
have floated from your present realm to the more pleasant place where life unfolds however you see fit. So what
is it today? A bright meadow with blue skies and a nice
picnic spread before you? A late evening conversation
where *this* time you convey your heart? Or that ideal is-
land, palm trees swaying, shaded beach chair calling? The
options are as endless as your imagination, because that's
the reliable vehicle that can always take you wherever you
want to go.

But as your mind wanders, wonder at its amazing, unseen-by-others power. What could possibly be the point of it? It's like God's perfect gift to give us a glimpse beyond this world to a more perfect place. It's His hint of heaven, planted in our thoughts, that He plans to show us in person one day. So carry on, dreamer! It's your appetizer of glory God has given to the one He loves!

No one's ever seen or heard anything like this, never so much as imagined anything quite like it—what God has arranged for those who love him.

1 CORINTHIANS 2:9–10 MSG

I like nonsense, it wakes up the brain cells. Fantasy is a necessary ingredient in living, it's a way of looking at life through the wrong end of a telescope. Which is what I do, and that enables you to laugh at life's realities.

DR. SEUSS

DEEPLY ROOTED

*I am the vine, you are the branches; he who abides in Me and I in him, he
bears much fruit, for apart from Me you can do nothing.*

JOHN 15:5 NASB

Have you ever wondered what trees would look like if they
didn't grow upward? Any other direction, with the exception of their branches, would just look weird. More
than that, they would crowd each other out and probably
topple over. God crafted His plant creation to point toward the sky and soak up the sun. And secretly, roots go
down to steady and nourish the growth.

Just like the trees, God has made you to grow upward
toward Him. As you turn your face toward His radiant
light, your whole soul surges with inexplicable energy.
Every branch of your life reaches out to feel His warmth
as the fruit of your God-chemistry blooms for all to see.

But your roots are just as important. Going down deep into God's Word, believing and living it, you are steadied for whatever storm life blows your way. You are nourished by God, satisfied and strengthened by the Source of all life itself. As you trust Him and get to know Him better, you will branch out into all the goodness God has planned for you.

He will be like a tree firmly planted by streams of water, which yields its fruit in its season and its leaf does not wither; and in whatever he does, he prospers.

PSALM 1:3 NASB

As the chaos swirls and life's demands pull at me on all sides, I will breathe in God's peace that surpasses all understanding. He has promised that He would set within me a peace too deeply planted to be affected by unexpected or exhausting demands.

WENDY MOORE

FREEDOM RINGS

❧ ⚜ ❧

Christ has set us free to live a free life. So take your stand!

GALATIANS 5:1 MSG

Blankets and lawn chairs litter the grass. Crowds have gathered from every corner of the county, ready for the late-night revelry. Music, playing from some unseen source, pierces the dark night sky. Soon another shrill sound is heard…climbing, a light ascending, and then *pow!* Explosions of brilliant red, gold, and blue fill the sky. *Ohhh*, whispers the awestruck crowd. Soon the sensation builds as color and sparkle and heart-pounding power punches through the darkness, the brilliant display cascading over the crowds. *Ahhh*, they say again. Fireworks show in vivid display how we Americans feel about our freedom.

But in the celebration, let the sounds of freedom sink even deeper. Let the lights color your thoughts as you realize that soul freedom runs beyond a soldier's work. God is able to free you from sadness so that you can celebrate life. To see His display of power and feel the pulse of divine pleasure toward you pounding in your heart. You are God's glorious firework, more spectacular than any grand finale. Let the wonder of His gift of freedom ring for all to hear!

So if the Son sets you free, you will be free indeed.

JOHN 8:36 NIV

Because You live, O Christ, the spirit bird of hope is freed for flying, our cages of despair no longer keep us closed and life-denying.

SHIRLEY ERENA MURRAY

MAGIC MOMENT

—◆———◆—

The God-begotten are also the God-protected. The Evil One can't lay
a hand on them. We know that we are held firm by God.

1 JOHN 5:18 MSG

Long months have passed in planning. Then the pain.
The anxious rush to the hospital, all minds flooded
with eager anticipation. And at last arrives that magic moment when a miracle cry fills the room and floods your
heart with newborn love. Wrinkly soft, sweet skin nestles
against your weary frame. For the first time, your eyes
meet with baby, and wild wonder fills your soul. You hold
life's greatest gift in your hands, the inexplicable treasure
of God-glory entrusted to your care.

In that moment, see yourself as that small child.
Imagine God, your Father, cradling you in His heavenly

arms, looking down in divine delight as your eyes meet. For He *is* holding you, even now. And He has imagined all the good that is yet to come—in this world, yes, but also in the one to come. God, who has given you new life and brought you into this world, is delighted you're here. Thrilled with the touch of your hand, your upward gaze into His face. Awed with your existence. He knows you are fragile and frail, totally dependent on His tender care. Do you?

So rest, little one, and snuggle in close (even as you go about your busy day). You couldn't be in better hands.

The gracious hand of our God is on everyone who looks to him.

Ezra 8:22 niv

God's friendship is the unexpected joy we find when we reach for His outstretched hand.

Janet L. Smith

BUNDLED WITH LOVE

❦ ⸺ ⸻ ⸺ ❧

He gathers the lambs in his arms and carries them close to his heart.

ISAIAH 40:11 NIV

For the umpteenth day, it's gray and dreary outside. Trees have long lost their leaves, and their bare, stark skeletons now sway and moan in protest as winter winds bend their frames. But inside, not so. The fireplace crackles and fires with light as you snuggle deeper into the soft, warm blanket bundled around you. The heat on your face reaches down to your toes and you savor the cozy softness of life, and smile.

God is smiling, too. His arms of love are the blanket wrapped around you. The touch of His hand is the warmth on your face. The soul satisfaction of life is His sweet gift filling you, warming you, head to toe. God wants to cover you with His love. Shelter you from the cold, bitter world outside. And He wants to cozy up to you, right there on your couch, celebrating your moment of comfort and peace. Lean into Him and let His fire light your soul. No matter what the season, you can always be wrapped in His love.

The eternal God is your refuge, and underneath are the everlasting arms.

DEUTERONOMY 33:27 NKJV

The impetus of God's love comes from within Himself, to share with us His life and love. It is a beautiful, eternal gift, held out to us in the hands of love. All we have to do is say, "Yes!"

JOHN POWELL, S. J.

GOD GIVE ME JOY
IN THE COMMON THINGS:

In the dawn that lures, the eve that sings.

In the new grass sparkling after rain,

In the late wind's wild and weird refrain.

GOD GIVE ME HOPE FOR

each day that springs,

God give me joy in the common things!

THOMAS CURTIS CLARK

MADE FOR MORE

❦ ⸺ ❧

In his kindness God called you to share in his eternal glory
by means of Christ Jesus.

1 PETER 5:10 NLT

Walk into an arcade and just watch it happen. Kids every-where are putting in their tokens, playing games, and collecting tickets as their prize. Amass enough, and they're ready to cash in at the counter, choosing from a selection of dollar-store treasures. As a parent, you marvel over their motivation, maybe even chuckle over their childishness. *They don't know what real treasure is*, you think to yourself, as you consider how much loftier your own ambitions are.

But God has a hidden message in that pleasure place. You were made for much more joy and delight than this present world—as wonderful as it is—could ever afford. God has given you this great big beautiful world, not to settle in forever, but to prick your wonder at what is yet to come! Every sunset, every mountain, every moment we enjoy on God's green earth is just the prelude to the symphony of pleasure waiting to be heard and experienced in heaven with Him. You, God's greatest prize, will find your deepest delight in the heart of where He is.

He has made everything beautiful in its time.
Also He has put eternity in their hearts.

ECCLESIASTES 3:11 NKJV

Our Creator would never have made such lovely days,
and have given us the deep hearts to enjoy them, above and beyond all
thought, unless we were meant to be immortal.

NATHANIEL HAWTHORNE

ON YOUR SIDE

My help comes from the LORD, the Maker of heaven and earth.

PSALM 121:2 NIV

You've seen it played out on the football field. Athletes who are supposed to be gearing up for the next play suddenly turn to face the crowd. Throwing their hands up and up, you realize they're sending a signal to you, the fans. *Get louder! Cheer us on! Distract our opposition!* they're telling you. And somehow, simply by hearing and knowing that people are for them, momentum changes. They get the ball back, drive it down the field, and score.

It just helps to know that you're not alone in your efforts. That someone believes in you, is for you, and is cheering you on.

God wants you to know He is your greatest fan. He has studied your plays and knows your routine. He knows what energizes you and what gets you down. He reads you better than any playbook. You are a star on His team, and He wants you to win every time.

So ignore the jeers from the opposing side. Listen for the voice of God, who has given you the victory, cheering you on (no matter how many times you may fumble the ball)! If God is for you, who can be against you? God doesn't have any losers on His team. He can make you a champion through Jesus Christ.

If God is for us, who can be against us?

ROMANS 8:31 NIV

Grasp the fact that God is for you—let this certainty make its impact on you in relation to what you are up against at this very moment; and you will find in thus knowing God as your sovereign protector... both freedom from fear and new strength for the fight.

J. I. PACKER

RISE AND SHINE

❦ ⟶ ⟵ ❦

For God is sheer beauty, all-generous in love, loyal always and ever.

PSALM 100:5 MSG

Esther could have let her coronation go to her head. After all, Persia's king chose her, a young Jewish girl, to be his queen over all the other women in the kingdom. Most people in her place would have worked the position for self-centered interests. But Mordecai, her cousin, urged her down a different path. The Jews were in real danger, he said, and she had the power to do something about it. God hadn't just granted her a crown. He had given her a purpose. So Esther sought the king's help and saved all her people. It's quite a spectacular story.

But the regal tale is not Esther's only. It's also yours. Though you feel no crown on your head, you sense

God's royal purpose for you in your heart. You were made for this very moment. Before time began, God planned your life on earth for a very specific purpose. You have the choice to bring beauty and hope to every person God places in your path. At the grocery store, ballpark, church, or work, you carry the grace of God's kingdom with you.

Like Esther, will you rise to the occasion and let God's glory shine through you?

The Sunrise from on high will visit us, to shine upon those
who sit in darkness...to guide our feet into the way of peace.

LUKE 1:78—79 NASB

We have missed the full impact of the gospel
if we have not discovered what it is to be ourselves, loved by God,
irreplaceable in His sight, unique among our fellow men.

BRUCE LARSON

LEMONADE CHEMISTRY

*God's love has been poured out into our hearts
through the Holy Spirit, who has been given to us.*

ROMANS 5:5 NIV

It seems an unlikely pairing: the acidic, sour lemon and the sweetness of sugar. Yet the recipe is so simple. Blended together, with the right amount of water, you have the world's best summer thirst quencher, the sour-but-sweet satisfaction your parched body craves. It's a universal sensation, and the truth behind it is, too. Opposites not only attract, but they often offer life a richer, better flavor.

So what would you say is the lemon in your life? Do you think your personality's too strong or bland? Your hair too curly or straight? Your bank account or talent pool too empty? No matter who the person, everyone has areas that just seem too sour to taste. But here's the miracle. Mixed with the sweetness of God's love for you, something magical happens. His strengths and your weaknesses blend to make a better life flavor than any summer ever saw. His presence literally reconfigures your chemical composition, and you become one cool drink for a dry and thirsty world. So the next time you taste a sour moment in your life, look up to God and smile.

It's His invitation to drink in and pour out His love.

He has said to me, "My grace is sufficient for you,
for power is perfected in weakness."

2 CORINTHIANS 12:9 NASB

We must drink deeply from the very Source
the deep calm and peace of interior quietude and refreshment
of God, allowing the pure water of divine grace to flow
plentifully and unceasingly from the Source itself.

MOTHER TERESA

HAPPY BIRTHDAY

*I tell you, there is joy in the presence of the angels of God
over one sinner who repents.*

LUKE 15:10 NASB

At this age, you try to brush it off. Act like it's no big deal. It's just another birthday, right? But inside, your inner child is giddy with anticipation. *Who's going to remember? What special surprises await my day?* And so you succumb to your mind's delight and indulge in whatever treat comes your way. *No diet today*, you smile as someone slides you a piece of cake. It's just time to celebrate!

Did you know that God is celebrating you, too? Not only because you were born on this earth but also because the world would not be the same without your unique personality. You have something to add, something to do, that no one else can. Every day is a new opportunity to see and celebrate the trust God has put in you.

Don't worry. The wrappings may look different than your average gift, but God has hidden surprises in every corner of your life, waiting for you to open and discover just how well He knows you, loves you, and has purposed every part of your life for good.

So dig in! Today is your day to celebrate a wonderful life with your loving God!

The father said to his slaves, "Quickly bring out the best robe and put it on him, and put a ring on his hand and sandals on his feet; and bring the fattened calf, kill it, and let us eat and celebrate; for this son of mine was dead and has come to life again; he was lost and has been found." And they began to celebrate.

LUKE 15:22–24 NASB

Our hunger for significance is a signal of who we are and why we are here, and it also is the basis of humanity's enduring response to Jesus. For He always takes individual human beings as seriously as their shredded dignity demands, and He has the resources to carry through with His high estimate of them.

DALLAS WILLARD

SPEED OF LIGHT

*Do not forget this one thing, dear friends: with the Lord a day is like
a thousand years, and a thousand years are like a day.*

2 PETER 3:8 NIV

Did you know that the earth, right now, is spinning
1,040 miles per hour (measured from the equa-
tor; it's a good bit slower if you live on the North
or South Pole). And you, with all of your busy to-
dos, are hurtling through space at breakneck speed,
even while spinning like a never-ending top. But we
never feel the motion, thanks to gravity—and a very
creative God who has a way of handling space and time.

But the facts reveal a deeper truth. Life as we perceive it is not always what it seems. There are forces much
greater and stronger than you constantly carrying you
through life. God, in His infinite wisdom and love for
you, has told you through space—and the time He came

into the world—that He has a hidden world of power and purpose surrounding your sensational life.

Today may look like an ordinary day to you, but the God of the unseen world is working faster than the speed of light to make all things work for your good, for every moment of your life in this world to reflect His amazing power and glory. There is no normal. Only spectacular life lived in the knowledge of His mighty power.

When I look at the night sky and see the work of your fingers—the moon and the stars you set in place—what are mere mortals that you should think about them, human beings that you should care for them?

PSALM 8:3–4 NLT

The beauty of the earth, the beauty of the sky, the order of the stars, the sun, the moon...their very loveliness is their confession of God: for who made these lovely mutable things, but He who is Himself unchangeable beauty?

AUGUSTINE

DIVINE REFLECTIONS

—◆———ᴜᴜᴜ———⟡—

For now we see only a reflection as in a mirror; then we shall see face to face.
Now I know in part; then I shall know fully, even as I am fully known.

1 CORINTHIANS 13:12 NIV

What would your ideal body be? What would you currently have to rearrange to achieve that image? If you're having trouble coming up with ideas, just check out the latest magazines lining the grocery store check-out. Or step into your local gym and marvel at the time, energy, and myriad of ways people work to shape or keep their body image. Image sculpting is a major phenomenon in our culture.

You, however, were created to be more. Better than the most beautiful magazine model. More impressive than the biggest bodybuilder. You were made to bear the image of God.

When you look at yourself in the mirror, you see the reflection of someone whose unique make-up tells a much bigger story. You have a Creator who has formed you to think, love, speak, play, feel, see, smell, and taste, just like Him. There is no other creature on earth like you. No one who bears the beautiful imprint your unique soul brings to this world. You are an expression of God like no other, with an even greater glory yet to be revealed when you are fully perfected in Christ.

So the next time you notice how much more buff that other person's body is, remember your divine reflection. Revel in the truth that you are a unique image-bearer of Christ, and you wouldn't trade that look for anything in the world!

When God created human beings, he made them to be like himself.

GENESIS 5:1 NLT

All that we have and are is one of the unique and never-to-be repeated ways God has chosen to express Himself in space and time.

BRENNAN MANNING

PURR-FECTION

Surely the arm of the LORD is not too short to save,
nor his ear too dull to hear.

ISAIAH 59:1 NIV

Turn on your TV to a National Geographic feature and you'll find the most ferocious felines, mercilessly stalking their prey. Even in a trip to the zoo, you're grateful for the bars and fences that keep you separated from the lions and tigers that, while beautiful, also boast a roaring fury that reminds you just how wild, powerful, and not-so-friendly they are.

But back at home, the animal kingdom seems quite different. Tired after a long day, you plop on the couch, and soon your cat comes crawling into your lap, purring with contentment. He's glad you're home, and happy to snuggle close. Sidling up to a scratch under the chin, his satisfaction sends you an inexplicable feeling of comfort, too.

It isn't just the cat nudging you. God wants to get your attention, too. Though the world may be filled with strong and often scary situations, God is powerful enough to tame them. Like the love of a sweet cat in your lap, God softens some of the hard things in life so that we can enjoy peace and love, even in a dangerous world. You don't need bars or fences like those at the zoo to separate yourself from the bad. God is your protector, the One who calms the seas and tames the cats to soften your heart and open your eyes to His comforting love.

The men were amazed and asked, "What kind of man is this? Even the winds and the waves obey him!"

MATTHEW 8:27 NIV

The longer I live, the more my mind dwells upon the beauty and the wonder of the world.

JOHN BURROUGHS

YOUR LOVE,

Lord, reaches to the heavens,

your faithfulness to the skies.

Your righteousness is like the highest mountains....

How priceless is your unfailing love, O God!

PSALM 36:5-7 NIV

MOUNTAIN HIGH

❦ ———⟡⟡⟡——— ❦

I love those who love me, and those who seek me find me.

PROVERBS 8:17 NIV

You can't get it from a photograph, though it gives a glimpse. You can't feel it from above, because airplanes alter the effect. Standing at the base of a mountain, you begin to understand. But it takes a climb, the effort exerted in search of the spectacular if you really want your eyes to see—all your senses to absorb—the impact of the mountain peak. At last on top, your breath gives way as you survey the enormity of God's amazing earth, the power of seeing from on high. The dizzying truth of your own smallness engulfs you like the expansive sky above.

But you know God is bigger. The Creator who wrought the ridges and told the seas to stay stands with you on that mountain and whispers through the swirling wind, *I made this for you.* Ecstatic at your awestruck wonder, He waits for you to realize the enormity of His love, the grandeur of His pleasure and power. You are His, the pinnacle of His creation. And He planned the mountain peak to speak of love. *His* love, grander and greater than anyone can conceive—revealed to those who climb to see.

Come, and let us go up to the mountain of the LORD...and he will teach us of his ways, and we will walk in his paths.

MICAH 4:2 KJV

Imagine what Israel and all of us who worship Israel's God would have missed if they had gone by the short route— the thrilling story of the deliverance from Egypt's chariots when the sea was rolled back. Let's not ask for shortcuts. Let's keep alert for the wonders our Guide will show us.

ELISABETH ELLIOT

SHOOTING STAR

— ✦ —

*The eyes of the LORD search the whole earth in order to
strengthen those whose hearts are fully committed to him.*

2 CHRONICLES 16:9 NLT

There you are, lying flat on your back (preferably
with a blanket beneath), out in the middle of no-
where. Far from the reach of city lights, the dark ex-
panse of midnight, moonless sky stretches before
your eyes. Twinkling stars dot your view. Cool dew
from the night air settles on your skin as you wait.
And wait. And wait. Flashing lights first excite, then
disappoint, as an imposter plane flies out of sight.

But then it comes. Streaking across the night sky, just
in the corner of your field of vision. A shooting star! Okay,
a meteor, if you must. But you saw it, the brilliant burst of

glory breaking through deepest heaven to brighten your world for the briefest moment. And you smile.

Why do you strain to see something beautiful, even for an instant? Because like Father, like child. The God who made you and named the stars watches and waits for you to catch the fire of His love—and then run with it through a darkened world. Your excitement, your pleasure, your passion for Him brightens the night and God's smiling face. You are a wonder to behold, a secret treasure worth searching the skies to see. Ignited by love, you light the universe with God's glory.

Then you will shine among them like stars in the sky
as you hold firmly to the word of life.

PHILIPPIANS 2:15–16 NIV

Lord, take my lips, and speak through them; take my mind,
and think through it; take my heart, and set it on fire.

WILLIAM H. H. AITKEN

HOLDING HANDS

*GOD promises to love me all day,
sing songs all through the night! My life is God's prayer.*

PSALM 42:8 MSG

You weren't expecting it. But suddenly, your special someone has slipped a hand into your own. The sensation of soft warmth seems to radiate from that touch up your arm and into your heart, warming you from head to toe. Like LEGO pieces made to lock, you find your fingers fit perfectly into the spaces around theirs, and you realize: you were both made for connection.

And it's true. Every aspect of your being confirms the fact that God made you (and everyone else) to need and enjoy the beauty of being loved. Of knowing that you're not alone.

But even when your hands can't find another's to hold, God is holding you. Like your fingers, your soul is shaped perfectly to receive Him and enjoy the waves of warmth and joy He radiates into every area of your life.

Every hug, every squeeze, every touch you feel in your physical body is God's tangible reminder of the unseen connection holding you deep in your heart. You are never alone. You are made for connection…and the God who made and loves you will keep you that way.

The LORD directs the steps of the godly. He delights in every detail of their lives. Though they stumble, they will never fall, for the LORD holds them by the hand.

PSALM 37:23–24 NLT

God's fingers can touch nothing but to mold it into loveliness.

GEORGE MACDONALD

BY FIREFLY LIGHT

❧ ———— ❧

Mary treasured up all these things and pondered them in her heart.

LUKE 2:19 NIV

The sun has nearly set and the hazy, hot day of summer slowly fades to dusky dark. Cicadas in hidden places clamor in crescendo effect, signaling the coming of night. But there it is! The other telltale sign of summer. Better get out your glass jars. The fireflies have taken flight.

For a brief moment, the world is a fairy land. Bright bursts of little lights glow on and off, always in the most unexpected places. Though they tease overhead, you wait for the lower lights and run to find the curious creature with this most coveted ability. Inevitably, it has floated on, flown somewhere else to light the sky, your imagination, and your determination to capture at least one for the jar that will house him for the night. You want to keep the wonder as long as you can.

And so God speaks to you by firefly light. Keep His wonder as long as you will. Just like the firefly lights in the most unexpected times and places, God delights to brighten your world with tiny glimpses of His glory and love. But you must learn to look, to watch, and to run after His heart with all you have, and hold His love luminaries captive with child-like wonder.

The kingdom of heaven is like treasure hidden in a field.

MATTHEW 13:44 NIV

The best things are nearest...light in your eyes, flowers at your feet, duties at your hand, the path of God just before you.

ROBERT LOUIS STEVENSON

FOREVER LOVE

Fear not, for I am with you;
Be not dismayed, for I am your God.
I will strengthen you,
Yes, I will help you,
I will uphold you with My righteous right hand.

ISAIAH 41:10 NKJV

Y ou couldn't help but notice the old, hunched-over man shuffling down the sidewalk. Beside him walked his aging wife, white hair framing years of life etched in wrinkles on her face. And then the flash. A youthful look of love darts from his life-lit eyes. And she smiles back, leaning down to take his hand. And so they walk past as you watch and wish, *I want a love that lasts like that.*

Of course you do. You were uniquely made to love—not for a moment but forever. But all around, from tabloid news to church prayer requests, you hear the stories of fractured homes and broken relationships. Rare glimpses into lifelong love like you just saw seem the stuff of ages past or fairy tales altogether.

But it isn't so. God put eternal love in your heart because you are designed for Him. From the moment you were born, through the days of your youth, and until your dying day, God strolls with you, side by side. Carries you, even, through the times of life. See the life-lit look of love in His eyes in the beauty of the world He has made for you. Reach up and take His hand, knowing His love will last your lifetime and beyond.

Even to your old age and gray hairs I am he, I am he who will sustain you. I have made you and I will carry you; I will sustain you and I will rescue you.

ISAIAH 46:4 NIV

In His arms He carries us all day long.

FANNY J. CROSBY

SUNRISE DANCE

From the rising of the sun to the place where it sets,
the name of the LORD is to be praised.

PSALM 113:3 NIV

A cool breeze brushes your face as you wait in anticipa-tion. Suddenly, a low glow, like a distant ember, burns a dark red on the horizon. Minute by minute, the fire grows, brilliant splashes of pink, orange, and red streak across the sky, and the clouds erupt in saturated color as if Paradise itself just broke into your world.

But after a few more mesmerizing moments, the glo-ry fades back to blue. It's time to face another day.

Yet something has changed inside you, ignited by the beauty your eyes beheld. Then the idea dawns: The same

God who swirled colors across the skies dances with you throughout your day! The spectacle isn't over. It has just begun, because the God of the sunrise paints beautiful moments into every area of your life, all day long. You just have to keep your eyes to the skies and look in anticipation for all the ways He colors your life with His love.

The heavens proclaim the glory of God.
The skies display his craftsmanship.

PSALM 19:1 NLT

To be grateful is to recognize the Love of God
in everything He has given us—and He has given us
everything. Every breath we draw is a gift of His love,
every moment of existence is a gift of grace.

THOMAS MERTON

OCEAN VIEW
[OR MICROSCOPIC MIRACLES]

It seems you've worked a million hours just for this
moment. Beach chair unfolded, you sit back—toes in
sand—and feel the world's weight melt off your shoul-
ders as the sun streams down. A sigh of release escapes
your lips as you survey the ocean's enormity before you.
So much power, beauty, and simplicity rolled into one
magnificent creation! It swells and retreats in rhythm
with your soul.

It's hard to imagine that underneath that mighty calm
and rhythmic beauty teems a world of writhing, crawling,
swimming, spinning creatures of every kind imaginable.
From the enormous blue whale to the almost infinite
number of microscopic plankton, God has packed His

water world with a living creativity we may never even see. But God does. Not a single microbe dances without His delight. Not a fish swims to a place God cannot see. He is everywhere, in control of all He has made. And He is with you, right where you are in your chair, enjoying His world of creativity.

Sometimes it takes an ocean view to get a glimpse of God's enormous glory. To grasp His ability to hold your life in the rhythmic beauty of His eternal purpose. His seas remind your soul to breathe. To survey His power to sustain that world—and your own—in perfect peace.

If I take the wings of the morning,
And dwell in the uttermost parts of the sea,
Even there Your hand shall lead me,
And Your right hand shall hold me.

PSALM 139:9–10 NKJV

Love comes while we rest against our Father's chest.
Joy comes when we catch the rhythms of His heart.
Peace comes when we live in harmony with those rhythms.

KEN GIRE

THE HEALER

He heals the brokenhearted and binds up their wounds.

PSALM 147:3 NIV

Nope. There's nothing pretty about it. In a moment of absentmindedness (or recklessly trying to relive your youth), you've gone and gotten hurt, the raw pain of scratched skin reminding you of other similar indiscretions in your past. But experience tells you something else, too. The pain won't be permanent. God wired our bodies with an amazing ability to heal themselves—to signal all the right cells to fight off infection, block blood flow, and regrow, smoothing over the rough places.

It isn't attractive, but it is most effective. It's God's hint to you that you were made to be whole. More than that, that He is your healer—not just of bumps and bruises on your skin but even the deep, gaping wounds of your soul. It's in His blood to repair, renew, just like He put that ability in your body. You were not meant to walk around wounded. He delights in making right all the rough places in your life, whether or not your own carelessness was the cause. You were made to live well, to be whole. Let the healing power of God's love work His wonder in your raw wounds, and marvel in His glorious gift of healing grace.

I am the LORD, who heals you.

EXODUS 15:26 NIV

The goodness of God is infinitely more wonderful
than we will ever be able to comprehend.

A. W. TOZER

IF WE ARE
CHILDREN OF GOD,

we have a tremendous treasure in nature and will realize that it is holy and sacred. We will see God reaching out to us in every wind that blows, every sunrise and sunset, every cloud in the sky, every flower that blooms, and every leaf that fades.

OSWALD CHAMBERS

TASTING PARADISE

You prepare a table before me in the presence of my enemies;
You anoint my head with oil;
My cup runs over.

PSALM 23:5 NKJV

You can smell it the second you walk through the door of your favorite restaurant. The fragrance of freshly cut herbs and savory spices tickles your nose and taunts your taste buds as you sit down to peruse the menu. What an array of creative entrée pairings! So many delicious options! How will you ever choose? But you know that in this place, you can't go wrong. The first bite of your meal confirms it. You've found paradise—and you're eating it!

What is it about food? Why does it unite families and ignite all our senses? Fuel our bodies and feed our imaginations? Can you imagine what a flavorless world would feel like? Fortunately, God doesn't want us to find out. Instead, He floods us with food we love. Tastes that season our lives with joy. *But why?*

God wants to give our souls a taste of who He is. To fill our hearts with His savory sweetness. To satisfy every sense we have that God is indeed good. His creative pairings of life and love are designed to defy even our wildest imaginations. Taste and see that God is good. Partake of His kindness, and share His goodness with the hungry world around you.

Oh, taste and see that the LORD is good;
blessed is the man who trusts in Him!

PSALM 34:8 NKJV

For God is, indeed, a wonderful Father who
longs to pour out His mercy upon us, and whose majesty is so great
that He can transform us from deep within.

TERESA OF AVILA

GIFT OF GIGGLES

❦ ━━━ ⟶

A joyful heart is good medicine.

PROVERBS 17:22 ESV

Oh yes, he just said *that*. Your pastor, in the seriousness of presenting communion elements, told the congregation to come, partake of the elephants of grace. Quickly correcting himself, he tries to keep his composure, but you cannot. Burning in your stomach, reddening your face until you feel about to explode, the littlest giggle escapes your lips. But your body isn't done. No, in fact, apparently there's a flood of funny ready to flow, and you can't stop the deluge of delight. So, in full surrender, you laugh to your heart's content, secretly thankful for the unexpected release.

But why do we ever try to rein it in? Laughter is the

sound of God's love for us! His gift of giggles, wherever it arises, releases our souls to sense God's utter delight in us and the world He has made. Didn't He make us in His image? Don't we all love to laugh? Yes, even our giggles give us a glimpse of God's smiling pleasure in us, His wonder at all the wacky and funny things we do. When you smile and let the laughter rise up in you, you are letting your pleasure mingle with God's matching joy. So laugh to your soul's content, and enjoy the release of God's giggles as you lighten the load of an overly burdened world.

God has brought me laughter,
and everyone who hears about this will laugh with me.

GENESIS 21:6 NIV

Laughter is the sun that drives winter from the human face.

VICTOR HUGO

PUPPY LOVE

It doesn't matter what kind of day you've had. How good or bad you've been. Where you've gone. One thing you know for sure: when you walk through the door of your house, you're gonna be loved. Not the ethereal, hypothetical kind either. Your little puppy will bounce up and down, wagging in whole body excitement at your arrival. Have a seat and he's instantly in your lap, licking and wiggling and snuggling just to welcome his favorite person in the world.

Don't you wish everybody in life was like your dog? To be sure, a little more wagging and less whining would brighten everybody's day. But the truth is, most of what you do seems uncelebrated and even unnoticed. At times, you wonder what value your life brings to the world's table.

Let your puppy's love lick you back to reality. God, who made your dog wriggle in visual delight, reminds you that He feels the same way about YOU. When you come home to God in your heart, all of heaven goes giddy with joy. It doesn't matter what kind of day you've had or what you've done. All is made right as He welcomes you to sit down and soak in His wild affection for you.

We love each other because he loved us first.

1 JOHN 4:19 NLT

You who have received so much love share it with others.
Love others the way that God has loved you, with tenderness.

MOTHER TERESA

YOU MAY
HAVE FORGOTTEN

or perhaps never have known how your heart shines like the sun against life's darkest nights—but it does. The God who made you sees it, and so do your friends. You matter to God and the people around you.... Remember how deeply you are loved.

JENNIFER GERELDS

NOTEWORTHY

❧ ⚌ ☙

*I write these things to you who believe in the name of the Son of God
so that you may know that you have eternal life.*

1 JOHN 5:13 NIV

You were expecting bills, the usual unwelcome intruder in your mailbox. Or maybe just a handful of advertising flyers, destined for the trash before you even walk back through the door. But today, there's a surprise. Hidden in the clutter is a clean white envelope, with your name and address handwritten in blue ink. Without even opening it, your heart gives a leap. *Someone is thinking about me!* you muse, as you drop all else to find out what they want to say. And you aren't disappointed. Inside, you read words that reveal a heart of love, an appreciation for you, and you are touched soul-deep. It's amazing how much words can matter.

God knows. He, who prompted your friend to write you this day, reminds you of His letter of love to you, waiting to be read. Yes, the God who spoke the world into being has taken the time to record His reckless affection for you. He eagerly waits for you to open His words every day and feel the warmth of His steady presence and love. You are never alone. You are forever His, the focus of His gaze and expression of His glory.

Blessed are those who hear it and take to heart what is written in it.

REVELATION 1:3 NIV

Take a moment to consider the awesome reality that the God who spoke and created the universe is now speaking to you. If Jesus could speak and raise the dead, calm a storm...and heal the incurable, then what effect might a word from Him have upon your life?

HENRY T. BLACKABY

MIND READER

Search me, O God, and know my heart; test me and know
my anxious thoughts. Point out anything in me that offends you,
and lead me along the path of everlasting life.

PSALM 139:23–24 NLT

Your closest friend has done it again, and it blows you away. "How do you know me so well?" you ask, marveling at how your friend always seems to know the best ways to make you smile. Of all the people in the world, only a select few really understand what makes you tick. But even those precious people still stand on the perimeter of what really goes on in your mind. Yes, they see more than most, but there still exists an inner sanctuary even the closest of friends can't enter.

Except God. The Designer and Creator of your brain knows every single thought in your head—even before you've thought it. No musing escapes His notice. No fleeting sadness or joy, jealousy or love, bravery or shame dawns on your soul without God seeing it. There, deep in your mind where no other human can see, God is there. He's listening to your heart's cry. Knowing the real you, and loving you like no other. Without a single spoken word, you have been heard and known by the King of all creation. Commune with Him there in the secret place and let the influence of His presence inform all that you are and do.

You have searched me, LORD, and you know me. You know when I sit and when I rise; you perceive my thoughts from afar.

PSALM 139:1–2 NIV

God is every moment totally aware of each one of us.
Totally aware in intense concentration and love....
No one passes through any area of life, happy or tragic,
without the attention of God with him.

EUGENIA PRICE

REAL ROMANCE

How precious to me are your thoughts, God! How vast is the sum of them!
Were I to count them, they would outnumber the grains of sand.

PSALM 139:17–18 NIV

You see it in the movies all the time. A couple falls in love. He is absolutely infatuated with her. She can't stop thinking about him. They are obsessed and delighted by even the thought of each other. It's just the way love goes.

But romance didn't start in Hollywood. It began with God, the author of love. Your view of that love, though, gets distorted in a myriad of ways, blurred in a broken world. But every now and then, in the purity of unadulterated affection, you get a glimpse of what real love looks like...a taste of just how passionate God feels—about you.

Did you know that God watches over you when you sit and when you rise? Where you sleep and when? He even knows what you're going to think before you think it! He protects you, provides for you, and prepares you for an incredible future with Him.

Before He even made the world, you were on His mind. While you were being knitted together inside your mom, He was thinking about you. His thoughts of you outnumber the sand. Now that's the heart of romance. All other tales simply pale by comparison.

He pays...attention to you, down to the last detail—
even numbering the hairs on your head!

MATTHEW 10:30 MSG

The God who created, names, and numbers the stars
in the heavens also numbers the hairs of my head....
He pays attention to very big things and to very small ones.
What matters to me matters to Him, and that changes my life.

ELISABETH ELLIOT

SOARING WITH EAGLES

—⁌ ⁕ ⁋—

The LORD doesn't see things the way you see them.
People judge by outward appearance, but the LORD looks at the heart.

1 SAMUEL 16:7 NLT

Did you know that certain eagles have the ability to see prey as small as a rabbit up to two miles away? Their incredible vision stems from the one million light cells per millimeter found on their retinas, five times more than we humans have. No matter how high they soar in the sky, they are keenly aware—and able to respond—to activity happening far below.

Did you also know that you share some of the same abilities as the majestic eagle? God has invited you to rise above the clamor of this world to heights where you can better hear His voice. Removed from distraction, your spiritual wings can unfurl and you can fly through life with all the divine insight you need to interpret the activity happening here on earth.

Do you feel the stress of this life? Have you ever wondered what was really going on? Don't stay bound to the ground, confined by the trappings of this world. God instead invites you to soar with Him, see life from His beautiful vantage point, and be ready to act in keen wisdom when He calls you to engage the world below.

Those who trust in the LORD will find new strength.
They will soar high on wings like eagles.
They will run and not grow weary.
They will walk and not faint.

ISAIAH 40:31 NLT

Because You live, O Christ, the spirit bird of hope
is freed for flying, our cages of despair
no longer keep us closed and life-denying.

SHIRLEY ERENA MURRAY

WILD BLUE YONDER

"As surely as my new heavens and earth will remain,
so will you always be my people,
with a name that will never disappear," says the LORD.

ISAIAH 66:22 NLT

When you were little, you wondered why you couldn't touch them. They seemed *sooo* close. Jumping up, you found those soft, cotton-candy clouds were still out of reach. So they left you to wonder, to dream about the stuff they're made of. Lying back on the green grass looking up into the wild blue yonder, the powder-white masses floated across the sky, filling your imagination as they morphed into shapes of animals or faces, like the heavens' moving picture show.

Of course, when you got older, you learned about evaporation and condensation, and the clouds lost a bit of their wonder-glory. With our adult, scientific mindset, we often miss their softer message, the invitation to imagine worlds beyond our own. Worlds where life is sweet and takes the form of all that's good. God whispers through the clouds, *Imagine My world to come!* As great as God's green earth already is, the glorious blue sky and beckoning clouds call us to consider where He has promised to take us—a place even more wonderful than our wildest imagination. He invites you to lie back and look up, knowing you are destined for greatness.

Your steadfast love, O LORD, extends to the heavens,
your faithfulness to the clouds.

PSALM 36:5 ESV

Lift up your eyes. Your heavenly Father waits to bless you—
in inconceivable ways to make your life
what you never dreamed it could be.

ANNE ORTLUND

READING RAINBOWS

❦ ⸺ ❦

Like the appearance of a rainbow in the clouds on a rainy day,
so was the radiance around him. This was the appearance
of the likeness of the glory of the LORD.

EZEKIEL 1:28 NIV

It's a moment of cognitive dissonance—the world when both sun and rain happen at the same time. A strange, ethereal hue paints the landscape as you search the skies for what you hope is there. And then you spot it! Faint at first, the sun's light scatters through the distant mist, breaking into brilliant color. Soon the rainbow arches across the sky, releasing its God-glory and the reminder of His promised protection.

Isn't it amazing how simple, white light refracts into a rainbow of color through the presence of rain? Like that raindrop, your life is backlit with the beautiful radiance of God's presence. Strange as it seems, it is through the rain—the rough places in our lives and souls—that God's light breaks forth into beautiful color. Without it, we'd never witness the wonder of the rainbow.

Rainy skies are no reason to doubt God's love or presence. He is simply waiting for the perfect moment to light your life and the world around you with a dazzling display of surprising hope for all the world to behold. Lit up by His love, you are God's rainbow reminder of promised grace, even when skies are gray.

Whenever the rainbow appears in the clouds,
I will see it and remember the everlasting covenant
between God and all living creatures of every kind on the earth.

GENESIS 9:16 NIV

God is the sunshine that warms us, the rain that melts the frost
and waters the young plants. The presence of God
is a climate of strong and bracing love, always there.

JOAN ARNOLD

FOREVER SPRING

He has made everything beautiful in its time.

ECCLESIASTES 3:11 NKJV

For months, bleak gray blanketed the earth. From any alien perspective, all would look lost in the barren, blank trees. Brown grass. Bitter winds. *What kind of world is this?* they'd say, not knowing what would come. But suddenly, pushing past the brown of earth, new blades of brilliant green grass burst forth. Out of seeming death itself, buds unfurl bright new foliage, washing the world in the vibrant colors of spring. Flowers and vines, birds and creatures of all kinds crawl and grow and give birth to the fragrance and vigor of life on this planet, the colorful expression of hope, love, and power from the One who has never failed to make it happen.

Every spring is a microcosm of God's miraculous work in you. Though you had no hope before, now you have been made new. Think not about the season before, the dreary skies and hindered hope. Trust that God, like spring, follows winter; God's hope, grace, and mercy follow trials. Believe it. Today, celebrate forever spring as you grow in the warmth of God's radiant love for you.

This means that anyone who belongs to Christ has become a new person. The old life is gone; a new life has begun!

2 CORINTHIANS 5:17 NLT

Above all, believe confidently that Jesus delights in maintaining that new nature within you, and imparting to it His strength and wisdom for its work.

ANDREW MURRAY

SALT SHAKER

❦ ——— ❧

Let your conversation be always full of grace, seasoned with salt, so that you may know how to answer everyone.

COLOSSIANS 4:6 NIV

At first taste, you know your soup's missing something. *Did I put in all the ingredients?* You double-check yourself, re-scanning the recipe. It looks right, but the taste is simply off. *Where is the kick?* you wonder. So you resort to seasoning. A little paprika and crushed cumin get it closer. Adding cilantro and pepper, you sense the victory coming. Finally, a squirt of lime and the right pinch of salt and voilà! Your dish has transformed from boring to bold, a savory sensation sure to delight even the pickiest appetite.

Sometimes life can be a lot like that pot of soup. All the ingredients for a good one are all around, but the overall flavor is just bland. But that's why God created you, God's seasoning packet. You may have never seen yourself like a salt shaker, but God does! He has filled you with His Spirit and pours you out in just the right places to add truth and love and mercy to His world. Suddenly, your life has seasoned the lives of everyone around you. The results are a savory delight that entices others to partake of God's goodness and a smile that lines your Father's face.

*Let me tell you why you are here. You're here to be
salt-seasoning that brings out the God-flavors of this earth.*

MATTHEW 5:13 MSG

*Savor little glimpses of God's goodness and His majesty,
thankful for the gift of them.*

TERESA OF AVILA

CELEBRATE GOD TIMES

*He is the one you praise; he is your God, who performed for you
those great and awesome wonders you saw with your own eyes.*

DEUTERONOMY 10:21 NIV

There's no way I can make it, you groan, glaring at the clock
that never rang your alarm. Your mind begins to race
with all the known obstacles that will make your on-time
arrival almost impossible. But you decide to give it a go
anyway. Then, to your amazement, you find open lanes
where traffic usually traps you in. Green lights urge you
on your way, and an open parking spot right in front
ushers you into your appointment—right on time.

Coincidences or luck? Some may think so. But if they
do, they miss God's marvelous smile. God, who parted
the water for Israel, parts traffic on the interstate, too.

God, who perfectly planned the world's creation, can certainly help you with your life's agenda. But the point isn't making your appointment. It's seeing the presence of God en route to it. It's realizing that no matter where you are going or what you are doing, you have the God of the universe at your side. Suddenly, your arrival seems much less significant, and the process of getting there a reason itself to celebrate. You are God's treasured companion, and you can relax. God's goodness always arrives right on time.

We humans keep brainstorming options and plans,
but GOD's purpose prevails.

PROVERBS 19:21 MSG

When I am with God my fear is gone; in the great quiet of God
my troubles are as the pebbles on the road,
my joys are like the everlasting hills.

WALTER RAUSCHENBUSCH

LOOK UP TODAY,

O parched plant, and open
your leaves and flowers for
a heavenly watering.

CHARLES H. SPURGEON

PENGUIN POUCHES

❦ ⚓ ❦

How priceless is your unfailing love, O God!
People take refuge in the shadow of your wings.

PSALM 36:7 NIV

Thank the Lord for penguin pouches. In the excruciating subzero temperatures of Antarctica, the fledgling flock of emperor penguins would perish in mere minutes. But tucked safely in the warmth of a mother's pouch, the fuzzy babies are free to grow, protected from all harm.

You, dear friend, are vulnerable like that baby bird. Left on your own to face the harsh elements of this world, your soul would freeze to death. Thank the Lord He has you hidden under His wing! That's right, God, who makes the emperor penguin and every other bird on earth, has painted a unique picture of His love and protection through our feathered friends. Just as they find shelter pressed up close under their parents' protective frame, so you were made to find strength in the shadow of the Almighty. He covers you completely from all harm and nestles you close to His heart so you can know His love. You are safe and sound, free to grow into all He has made you to be as you keep close to Him!

Whoever dwells in the shelter of the Most High
will rest in the shadow of the Almighty.

PSALM 91:1 NIV

Love is the sweet, tender, melting nature of God flowing
into the creature, making the creature most like unto Himself.

ISAAC PENINGTON

SOUNDS LIKE LOVE

❧ ⸱⸱⸱ ❧

Let everything that has breath praise the LORD. Praise the LORD!

PSALM 150:6 NIV

It's like a symphony warming up for a performance. Little finches herald the sun's first breaking rays. But as the day's light rises, so does the chatter of blue jays and robins, mockingbirds and sparrows. Dogs bark, crickets chirp, squirrels scold and scurry, while a host of other creatures join the chorus. Each sound unique, they blend together into the beautiful song of vibrant life on God's green earth.

Listen to the wonder. Each creature in creation lifts its voice as only it can. Contemplate their different calls to each other—to you. They are celebrating! God's world resounds with the joy of His creativity, the love of His presence with all He has made. Just imagine how different life would be without any noise. How empty the outside air would feel. Every day God gives you the privilege of front-row seats in this symphony of praise. He directs the melody to delight your ears and turn your sight to the sound's beautiful source: God Himself. Can you hear Him, too? Through the tunes of creation, God's love song is singing over you.

Deep calls unto deep at the noise of Your waterfalls;
All Your waves and billows have gone over me.
The LORD will command His lovingkindness in the daytime,
And in the night His song shall be with me

PSALM 42:7–8 NKJV

Does not all nature around me praise God? If I were silent, I should be an exception to the universe. Does not the thunder praise Him as it rolls like drums in the march of the God of armies? Do not the mountains praise Him when the woods upon their summits wave in adoration? Does not the lightning write His name in letters of fire? Has not the whole earth a voice? And...can I silent be?

CHARLES H. SPURGEON

GRACE LIKE RAIN

*The grace of our Lord was poured out on me abundantly,
along with the faith and love that are in Christ Jesus.*

1 TIMOTHY 1:14 NIV

One look overhead and you know what's going to happen. Those black, low-lying clouds are about to let loose. As if someone flipped a switch, suddenly the heavens open up to pour out a flood of warm, wonderful rain all over the dry earth beneath. And the ground is ready (even if you aren't) to soak up every drop, sending it to the roots of plants and trees, pooling it for birds and animals, and saving it for rivers and seas to spread the glory as far as it can go.

As annoying as it may seem when you've planned that outdoor activity, you have to watch in wonder. What would the world be like without water? You've seen the effects in desert regions. All green would be gone. Life, in all forms, would shrivel and die.

Why would God make His creation so dependent on one, miraculous element? Perhaps so you could see the same principle at work in your spirit. You need God as the land needs rain to grow and thrive. When you receive His life-giving love, you become a reservoir of grace, ready to flood the world with God's living water.

Ready to open up the sky? Believe that you are loved. God's grace pours down like rain to renew your hope and revive the lost world around you.

Be glad, people of Zion, rejoice in the LORD your God,
for he has given you the autumn rains because he is faithful.
He sends you abundant showers, both autumn and spring rains, as before.

JOEL 2:23 NIV

Grace means that God already loves us as much as
an infinite God can possibly love.

PHILIP YANCEY

APPLE DELIGHT

Show me the wonders of your great love....
Keep me as the apple of your eye.

What do you love more than anything in the world? God? Your family? Friends? Maybe a cold bowl of ice cream on a hot summer's day?

It's a hard question to answer sometimes because we use the word "love" so loosely. In the English language, the same word can be used to describe a million variations of love for someone or something.

You might have heard the good news that God loves you. And it's true—the Bible says it over and over. But sometimes you can miss the true meaning. Looking at your track record, or maybe even deeper into your heart, you might conclude that while God may love you (because He doesn't lie), He couldn't possibly like you very much. So you resign yourself to "being a good person."

But you've missed God's real message. He doesn't just love you. He likes you. He delights in you. And He wants deep intimacy with you right now where you are! You are the apple of God's eye, the one who brings a big smile to His face every time He sees you.

He encircled him, he cared for him, he kept him as the apple of his eye.

DEUTERONOMY 32:10 ESV

As the beloved of God, under the shadow of His wings—and as the apple of God's eye—the seeds of great faith live within us.

GARY SMALLEY AND JOHN TRENT

SHEEP STORY

*He tends his flock like a shepherd: He gathers the lambs
in his arms and carries them close to his heart.*

ISAIAH 40:11 NIV

What *was* God thinking when He compared His people
to sheep? Of all creatures! After all, sheep aren't the
smartest in the animal kingdom. When they fall over, they
need help to get up. In the absence of a leader, they'll
simply follow each other—even over a cliff. They frighten
easily. And they're easy prey for numerous predators—
unless a good shepherd is guarding them.

And then you begin to see God's point. Maybe sheep
can show us a thing or two about ourselves. Left to our own
devices, we really are a flock of foolish creatures destined
to make a mess of things outside of His direction.

Fortunately, you aren't on your own. God, your
Shepherd, is the very best in the business. He comforts
you with His gentle touch. He guards your life from

dangers in the distance. He leads you to graze on His grace and drink deeply of His calming love. And even when you wander from the fold, He doesn't leave you for the wolves. No, the Great Shepherd searches for every lost lamb until he is found, and carries him safely home.

You may feel sometimes like a lost and lonely lamb, but God never loses sight of His loved ones. Listen for His familiar voice and follow His footsteps. He always leads you home.

He calls his own sheep by name and leads them out....
His sheep follow him because they know his voice.

JOHN 10:3–4 NIV

God is the shepherd in search of His lamb. His legs are scratched,
His feet are sore, and His eyes are burning. He scales the cliffs and
traverses the fields. He explores the caves.
He cups His hands to His mouth and calls into the canyon.
And the name He calls is yours.

MAX LUCADO

WHITE AS SNOW

◆ ◆◆◆ ◆

Most important of all, continue to show deep love for each other,
for love covers a multitude of sins.

1 PETER 4:8 NLT

The kids are giddy with excitement, as if Christmas is coming tomorrow. Only the present they hope to open lies outside. Peering through the window at slate-colored skies and sterile ground, you wonder if the weather forecasters have gotten it right this time. But in next morning's light, you behold the miracle of answered hope. All that had been dark and dreary now gleams a brilliant white, a deep blanket of snow covering what seems like all of creation. Sparkling like mini diamonds in the light, the world seems brighter, cleaner, purer than you could ever imagine. And you marvel at how, in just mere moments, God could make the barren so beautiful.

And then you remember. *That's just who God is.* He's the one who brings life's beauty. In the wonder of snow, God whispers His power to whitewash your soul. No matter how bleak the landscape of your life has been, His cleansing forgiveness covers over all and creates an entirely new beautiful scene in its place. So when you see the snow, remember your soul. You can be just as clean and new. You can sparkle with the grace of God's love and forgiveness, shining down on you, brightening the world.

"Come now, and let us reason together," says the LORD,
"though your sins are like scarlet, they shall be as white as snow;
though they are red like crimson, they shall be as wool."

ISAIAH 1:18 NKJV

In His love He clothes us, enfolds us, and embraces us;
that tender love completely surrounds us, never to leave us.

JULIAN OF NORWICH

DATE WITH DESTINY

No eye has seen, no ear has heard, and no mind has imagined what God has prepared for those who love him. But it was to us that God revealed these things by his Spirit.

1 CORINTHIANS 2:9–10 NLT

What do you want to be when you grow up? It's the question your parents and teachers always wanted to know. As a kid, it was the stuff of dreams. Maybe one day you imagined you'd be the president. The next, a helpful doctor. Or a fireman. A famous ballerina. Or a vet. But as you got older, the question seemed less ethereal. Course choices were made. And ultimately, you found yourself outside of school, either working your way up to an anticipated destination or wandering along an unexpected path.

But God's children never grow too old to dream, because His ultimate plan for you lies beyond the parameters of this life. Your career here is not a destination or an identity. It's merely one of God's many chosen methods to make your heart, soul, and mind ready for the amazing glory that lies ahead.

Whether you're a CEO or a CCT (chief cleaner of toilets), you can embrace your duties with a thankful heart and mind filled with promise. You have a date with destiny—God Himself—who has adopted you as a royal member of His family. Your coronation day is coming.

Remember the things I have done in the past. For I alone am God! I am God, and there is none like me. Only I can tell you the future before it even happens. Everything I plan will come to pass.

ISAIAH 46:9–10 NLT

If you do not hope, you will not find what is beyond your hopes.

ST. CLEMENT OF ALEXANDRIA

CROWNING GOLD

~❦~

The LORD takes delight in his people; he crowns the humble with victory.

PSALM 149:4 NIV

Every four years, we gather around our TV sets (or maybe even get to go in person) to watch the Olympics. We gawk at muscles, marvel at ability, and strain in our seats to help our favorite person or team pull first through the finish line. For former athletes, the games rekindle the competitive fire we felt in our youth. The rest just watch in wonder at what it must feel like to win the gold. To be crowned winner of the world.

But you don't have to dream. God has already declared it by the intense training and work accomplished by His Son. No matter who you are, what you've done, how inadequate you feel, God has crowned you the winner in

His kingdom. Why? Because that's who He has made you to be. As His child, you are the most cherished of all His creation, the honored recipient of His love and grace.

So why cower in self-contempt or feel inferior to those who seem capable of greater feats? You have been given the place of prominence, the top-center step of life's Olympic ceremony. So wear your God-given gold with pride in His grace, and salute His goodness with the sound of your thanks.

I press on toward the goal to win the prize for which
God has called me heavenward in Christ Jesus.

PHILIPPIANS 3:14 NIV

The value of a person is not measured on an applause meter;
it is measured in the heart and mind of God.... Rest assured,
for on God's scale, the needle always reads high.

JOHN FISCHER

STANDING TALL

When you walk through the fire, you will not be burned; the flames will not set you ablaze. For I am the LORD your God, the Holy One of Israel, your Savior.

ISAIAH 43:2–3 NIV

The giant sequoia trees on California's coast have a secret to their unprecedented success as the tallest trees in the world. Some standing as tall as a twenty-five-story building, their massive trunks stretch over thirty feet in diameter. But that's where you find the secret's source. Soot darkens wide swaths of bark, harking back to the fiery blaze that burned across its path not long ago.

Oddly, fire—the one element that would seem to threaten their existence—actually aids their exponential growth. Over time, forest foliage, vines, and underbrush block out the sun and rain necessary for the sequoia's roots. Only a forest fire can clear the debris to create a way for greater growth.

God, the maker of the great sequoia, works the same wonder in the lives of His people. You may not see any point to the pain you have experienced in life. But somehow, through suffering, God clears away the wrong thoughts and distractions that make us spiritually malnourished. Though the heat may be hard to endure, keep standing strong. God is clearing the way for you to grow strong and tall, flourishing in His unfailing love.

Since we are receiving a kingdom that cannot be shaken,
let us be thankful, and so worship God acceptably with reverence and awe,
for our "God is a consuming fire."

HEBREWS 12:28–29 NIV

What can harm us when everything must first touch God,
whose presence surrounds us?

MAY HIS
FACE SMILE WITH
FAVOR ON US.

PSALM 67:1 NLT

TIME FOR PEACE

◈───────◈

In peace I will lie down and sleep, for you alone, LORD,
make me dwell in safety.

PSALM 4:8 NIV

Your alarm clock sounds, and another long day unfolds in your mind before your feet hit the floor. Considering the size of today's to-do list, you wonder how you're going to squeeze in time for a workout, not to mention time for friends, for family, for God.

So you start out with first things first. Pouring yourself a large cup of coffee, you curl up on the sofa and soak in the praise of Psalms, some wisdom from Proverbs, and a story from the Gospels. Suddenly, the tyranny of the urgent starts losing its hold in light of God's presence. You are known. Protected. Loved. Provided for. And the world's worries vanish as you enter the rest of your Father's care.

Now you are ready for the rest of the day. Not because you are now fueled up to go do it on your own, but because you are filled with the comfort of His presence as you go, and your spirit rests—regardless of the day's activity. You are assured that the God of glory you read about this morning will be just as glorious in your life today.

In God, there is no need for stress. He invites you to rest—not only in your eternal future but in every moment now, knowing He is sufficient for your every need today.

In vain you rise early and stay up late, toiling for food to eat—
for he grants sleep to those he loves.

PSALM 127:2 NIV

A quiet morning with a loving God puts the events
of the upcoming day into proper perspective.

JANETTE OKE

BACK STORY

❦ ⸺ ⟐ ⸺ ❧

I am your shield, your very great reward.

GENESIS 15:1 NIV

Surely David felt the pressure. All of Israel's army lined one mountain ridge, and the fierce, taunting Philistines faced them from the opposite side. Goliath, their tallest, strongest, and most experienced warrior, had walked forward with a daunting challenge: a one-on-one duel, winner takes all. Young shepherd-boy David was the only person daring enough to break from the ranks and enter the battlefield alone.

At least, that's how it appeared to everyone watching. But David knew he had secret company. The same God that had helped the shepherd fend off predators in the field walked with him now, ready to silence this rival, too. So David simply did what he had trained to do, and God shined His glory through a perfectly shot stone and an instantly dead enemy.

So what is your Goliath today? Problems with your bank account? Insurmountable family stress? Too many to-dos? Remember that the God who has gotten you this far still has your back. He is for you, loves you more than you can imagine, and stands ready to reveal His glory through you when you step forward in faith.

If God is for us, who can be against us?

ROMANS 8:31 NIV

God takes care of His own.... At just the right moment He steps in and proves Himself as our faithful heavenly Father.

CHARLES R. SWINDOLL

FLASH OF GLORY

Whatever the LORD pleases, he does, in heaven and on earth,
in the seas and all deeps. He it is who makes the clouds rise at the end
of the earth, who makes lightnings for the rain and brings forth his wind
from his storehouses.

PSALM 135:6–7 ESV

Did you know that a single bolt of lightning can raise the air temperature around it by as much as 50,000 degrees Fahrenheit?! That's more than a hundred million electrical volts, according to National Geographic, all funneled into one flashing force of nature, a brilliant display of power by the One who sent it.

The Bible says that God controls every lightning bolt and tells it where it should go. Can you imagine if you had that much power? So much that in a millisecond, you could change the face of the world and everything around it?

Has it struck you that you, as God's child, possess this powerful potential within you? You may not be ready to shoot lightning bolts at the world, but the God of the universe who creates and directs all the earth's massive energy has the ability to equip you with awesome power.

Every second, more than one hundred lightning bolts strike somewhere on our planet. Every one of them, blast after spectacular blast, should blow your mind. Like His bolts, God has charged you with a power more potent than the sun. Let Him release His brilliant glory through you today.

He covers his hands with the lightning and commands it to strike the mark.

JOB 36:32 ESV

O God, creator of light: at the rising of Your sun this morning,
let the greatest of all lights, Your love,
rise like the sun within our hearts.

OCTOPUS MANEUVERS

Come close to God, and God will come close to you.

JAMES 4:8 NLT

First, you notice it out of the corner of your eye. Ever since you opened the storybook, your child has been creeping closer to you. By page one, she's facing you, eyes full of anticipation. Page two finds her close by your side. But by page three, her foot has slipped over your lap and anchored itself on the other side. Like an octopus, she has managed to slink all other arms and legs under the outstretched book, until her body is full and center on your lap. Arms around her on either side as you hold the book in front, you can't help but smile as she snuggles in because you know: stories sound better when they're shared as close as possible.

Child of God, can you hear your heavenly Father reading your story? Every day that your life unfolds is another spectacular adventure filled with colorful characters and an enchanting, divine romance. It was written before the world for you to hear and experience today, perfectly plotted to delight, intrigue, and satisfy your soul. Will you settle for a distant read, like your child at page one? Or would you rather crawl up close next to God, your Creator, and revel in His love as you look at life together?

Don't wait for another page. His arms are open, waiting.

So let us come boldly to the throne of our gracious God. There we will receive his mercy, and we will find grace to help us when we need it most.

HEBREWS 4:16 NLT

God talks to those who humbly bring themselves before Him— young and old—to hear Him speak…. What do you lose by listening to the God who loves and lives today, who created man and moon and who wants to walk with you?

BECKY TIRABASSI

DIVINE BREATH

His purpose was for the nations to seek after God and perhaps
feel their way toward him and find him—though he is not
far from any one of us. For in him we live and move and exist.
As some of your own poets have said, "We are his offspring."

ACTS 17:27–28 NLT

You can't even see it with your eyes, but the magic is happening every moment you breathe. Oxygen, cool and clean, escapes from leaves all over the earth, the by-product of a photosynthetic process that makes plant life viable all over the globe. Fortunately for us humans, it's exactly the composition of air our lungs require to feed and fuel our bodies. Amazingly, the carbon dioxide we exhale is the critical compound feeding the photosynthetic process for plants. It's one incredible cycle that sustains life all over our beautiful planet.

It's also a picture of the unseen power feeding the soul of God's children. Every moment we live, every breath they take, we are taking in the very breath of God.

He surrounds us, filling us with energy and creativity that come from His divine source.

As you reach out to others, loving and making the world a better place, you can be breathing out the life you have been given. You can become an integral part of the process of God, the divinely orchestrated cycle of receiving and giving that graces His people and gives hope to the entire world.

So take a deep breath and thank the God of creation who fills your lungs and your soul with incredibly good things. Then feel His smile as you exhale, knowing you can keep the process going.

The wind blows wherever it pleases. You hear its sound,
but you cannot tell where it comes from or where it is going.
So it is with everyone born of the Spirit.

JOHN 3:8 NIV

We have been given the breath of life, designed with a unique,
one-of-a-kind soul that exists forever—whether we live it
as a burden or a joy or with indifference doesn't change the fact that
we've been given the gift of being, now and forever.

WENDY MOORE

MUSTARD SEEDS

*Now faith is confidence in what we hope for
and assurance about what we do not see.*

HEBREWS 11:1 NIV

Got a ruler? Look at the one-millimeter mark. That's the size of one mustard seed. Yet packed inside that ultra-tiny package is all the plant DNA needed to form roots and stems, leaves and flowers, and an amazing ability to convert sun and rain into daily sustenance. It certainly doesn't look impressive at first, but the mustard seed is packed with power that in time brings a colorful plant and seasons the earth with distinctive flavor.

Did you know that when you first believed God, He planted a seed in your soul? Not the kind for photosynthesis but for trusting God to produce great things through you. God has given each one of His kids the gift of faith in who He is and what He can do. Though it might not seem like a big deal, God says that tiny bit of trust in Him is packed with supernatural power you wouldn't believe. So big, in fact, that it can literally move mountains.

God didn't plant the seed of faith in you to stay small. He wants it to grow, giving color and flavor to the world where He planted you. What do you need to trust God to do today? Believe that He can move mountains, and watch in wonder as He grows a miracle—and your faith—right before your eyes.

For truly, I say to you, if you have faith like a grain of mustard seed,
you will say to this mountain, "Move from here to there,"
and it will move, and nothing will be impossible for you.

MATTHEW 17:20 ESV

Stay focused on God's ways and principles. Live every day in the
knowledge that He loves you and He is present within you, enabling you
to do mighty things for His kingdom.

GEORGE BARNA

MAY YOUR ROOTS

go down deep into the soil of God's

marvelous love; and may you be able

to feel and understand, as all God's

children should, how long, how wide,

how deep, and how high his love really is;

and to experience this love for yourselves,

though it is so great that you will never see the

end of it or fully know or understand it.

And so at last you will be filled up

with God himself.

EPHESIANS 3:17–19 TLB

IF YOU ENJOYED THIS BOOK
OR IT HAS TOUCHED YOUR LIFE
IN SOME WAY,
WE'D LOVE TO HEAR FROM YOU.

Please write a review at Hallmark.com,
e-mail us at booknotes@hallmark.com,
or send your comments to:

Hallmark Book Feedback
P.O. Box 419034
Mail Drop 100
Kansas City, MO 64141